I0796609

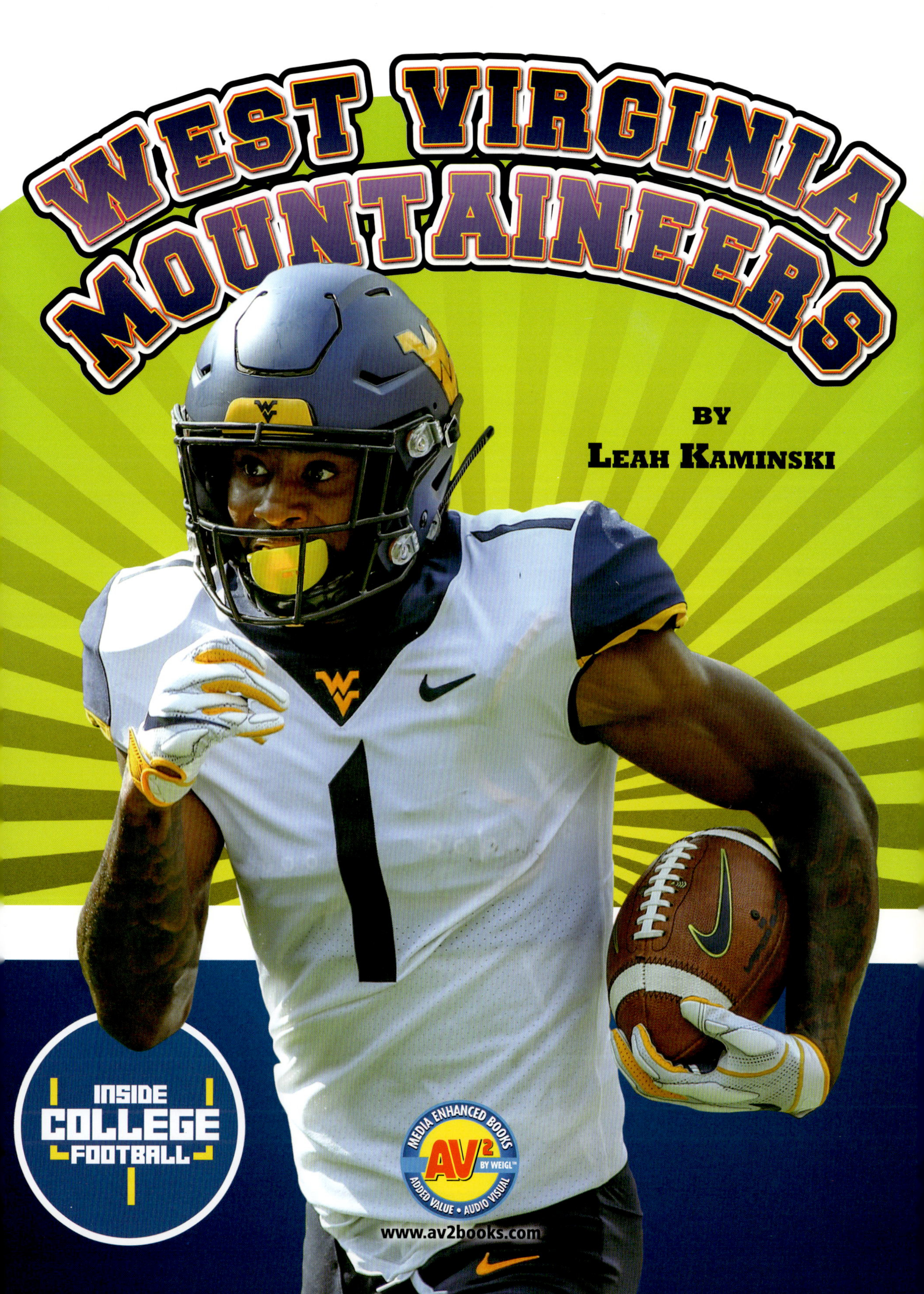
WEST VIRGINIA MOUNTAINEERS
BY
LEAH KAMINSKI
INSIDE
COLLEGE
FOOTBALL
MEDIA ENHANCED BOOKS
AV2
BY WEIGL
ADDED VALUE • AUDIO VISUAL
www.av2books.com

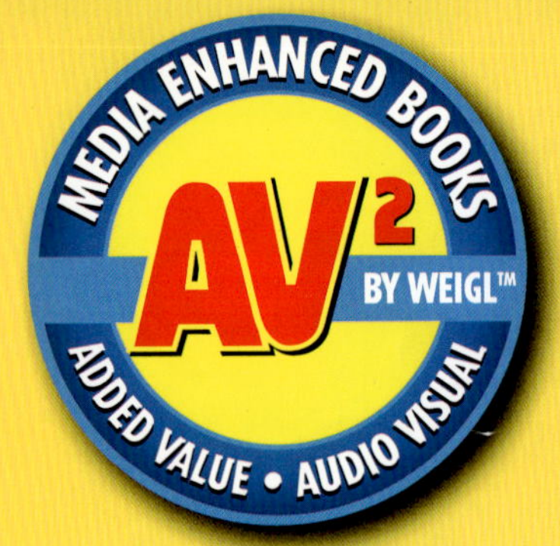

Go to **www.av2books.com**, and enter this book's unique code.

BOOK CODE

AVK34658

AV² by Weigl brings you media enhanced books that support active learning.

AV² provides enriched content that supplements and complements this book. Weigl's AV² books strive to create inspired learning and engage young minds in a total learning experience.

Your AV² Media Enhanced books come alive with...

Audio
Listen to sections of the book read aloud.

Key Words
Study vocabulary, and complete a matching word activity.

Video
Watch informative video clips.

Quizzes
Test your knowledge.

Embedded Weblinks
Gain additional information for research.

Slideshow
View images and captions, and prepare a presentation.

Try This!
Complete activities and hands-on experiments.

... and much, much more!

Published by AV² by Weigl
350 5th Avenue, 59th Floor
New York, NY 10118
Website: www.av2books.com

Library of Congress Control Number: 2018968220

ISBN 978-1-7911-0120-6 (hardcover)
ISBN 978-1-7911-0121-3 (multi-user eBook)
ISBN 978-1-7911-0122-0 (single-user eBook)

Printed in Guangzhou, China
1 2 3 4 5 6 7 8 9 0 23 22 21 20 19

042019
102318

Project Coordinator: Jared Siemens Designer: Terry Paulhus

Every reasonable effort has been made to trace ownership and to obtain permission to reprint copyright material. The publishers would be pleased to have any errors or omissions brought to their attention so that they may be corrected in subsequent printings.

The publisher acknowledges Alamy, Getty Images, and Wikimedia Commons as its primary image suppliers for this title.

West Virginia Mountaineers

CONTENTS

Introduction

The West Virginia University (WVU) Mountaineers are a National Collegiate Athletic Association (NCAA) Division I team. They have been playing football since 1891 and are part of the Big 12 Conference. The team has won the most games of any school that has not won a National Championship, with 752 games across 82 winning seasons.

West Virginia players have a history of individual successes, too. More than 180 Mountaineers have gone on to play in the National Football League (NFL). Since 2012, WVU has had the most first-round **draft** picks in the NFL Draft among Big 12 schools. There are 11 consensus **All-Americans** in Mountaineers history. "Consensus" means that every group that chooses All-American teams agrees on the quality of those players.

True freshman Leddie Brown finished the 2018 season as WVU's third-leading rusher. Brown logged 446 yards and four touchdowns in 11 games for the Mountaineers.

Under Head Coach Dana Holgorsen, the Mountaineers had seven winning seasons and two bowl wins. They finished second in the Big 12 in 2016 and competed in the Russell Athletic Bowl. The Mountaineers were one of the top 25 teams in the nation throughout the 2018 season.

Safety JoVanni Stewart dominated West Virginia's defense in the 2018 season. Stewart recorded 54 total tackles, including 38 solo tackles, 10.5 tackles for loss, and a fumble recovery.

WEST VIRGINIA

Stadium Mountaineer Field at Milan Puskar Stadium

Division Division I Football Bowl Subdivision, Big 12 Conference

Head Coach Neal Brown

Location Morgantown, West Virginia

National Championships 0

Nicknames Mountaineers, WVU

17 Bowl Games since 2000

9 10-Win Seasons

253 Nationally Televised Games

189 Players Drafted into the NFL

History

WVU came closest to a National Championship in 1988, with **Major Harris** as quarterback under the leadership of coach **Don Nehlen**.

The 1923 Mountaineers outscored opponents 297 to 41. Their 7-1-1 record included a tie game against rival Penn State.

WVU lost 72–0 in its first game against Washington and Jefferson College in 1891. The team did not play again for two years. Since then, the Mountaineers have been much more successful. They had their first undefeated regular season in 1922, including seven shutout games. A shutout game means that they did not allow the opponent to score any points. They also had undefeated regular seasons in 1988 and 1993.

The Mountaineers have several spirited **rivalries**, including the Backyard Brawl against the University of Pittsburgh, or Pitt. They also have a rivalry with Pennsylvania State University. In 1988, WVU defeated Penn State's Nittany Lions for the first time in 33 years. In a famous and exciting moment known as "The Play," quarterback Major Harris faked out Penn State and outran seven tacklers for a 26-yard touchdown. Harris's play led the Mountaineers to national recognition.

Tradition is important to the team. The players touch a piece of coal before entering the locker room to honor the miners of West Virginia. The team's entrance into the stadium is called the "Mountaineer Mantrip." It was named after the daily trip down into the mines taken by coal miners. "Gold Rush" is another tradition that encourages fans to come to games wearing the Mountaineers' golden yellow color.

Fourteen years after the University of West Virginia was founded, the Mountaineers played their first football game on a field that had previously been a cow pasture. In their first decade of play, the Mountaineers won just more than half of their games.

The Stadium

Morgantown becomes the largest city in the state of West Virginia when the stands at Milan Puskar Stadium are full. Mountaineers fans outnumber residents of the state's largest city, Charleston, by more than 10,000 people on game days.

West Virginia's first stadium, now referred to as Old Mountaineer Field, was built in 1924. Called "The Jewel of the Mountains," it was nestled in a natural valley. The stadium was relocated in 1980 and renamed Mountaineer Field. In 2004, the seating area was named after Milan Puskar, who donated $20 million toward **renovation** costs. Since then, the stadium has undergone several more renovations. Updates include wider concourses with murals highlighting Mountaineers **legends**. New luxury suites have also been added in recent years.

The construction of Touchdown Terrace brought the stadium's official capacity to 60,500. This building is attached to the stadium and offers several suites, an outdoor plaza, and other seating area options. The largest crowd to ever attend a game at the stadium was above the official capacity. On November 20, 1993, 70,222 fans watched WVU defeat the University of Miami. Fans are provided with pom-poms at home games, and musical cues tell fans when to wave them and make noise. The Pride of West Virginia, the WVU marching band, marches out in the shape of the state map. They start each game by playing the school's fight song, "Hail, West Virginia," and the classic "Take Me Home, Country Roads."

Mountaineer Field at Milan Puskar Stadium hosts a "Gold Rush" game each season. Fans dress entirely in gold, making the stadium glow with Mountaineer pride.

Where They Play

Welcome to Mountaineer Field at Milan Puskar Stadium, home of the West Virginia Mountaineers. More than 60,000 loyal fans form a sea of blue and gold as the Pride of West Virginia marching band plays. The team bursts through a cloud of smoke and runs onto the field to face its opponent while the crowd cheers. The Mountaineers are ready to dominate.

Arena
Mountaineer Field at Milan Puskar Stadium

Location
Morgantown, West Virginia

Broke Ground
1979

Completed
1980

Surface
Artificial Turf

Features
- High-definition video board measuring more than 3,500 square feet (325 square meters)
- Brohard Hall of Traditions with interactive displays and videos
- Legends Park honoring members of the Mountaineer Legends Society

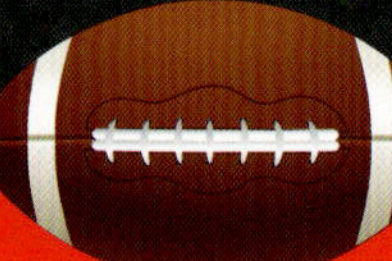

BIG 12

1. **Baylor University** *Waco, Texas*
2. **Iowa State University** *Ames, Iowa*
3. **Kansas State University** *Manhattan, Kansas*
4. **Oklahoma State University** *Stillwater, Oklahoma*
5. **Texas Christian University** *Fort Worth, Texas*
6. **Texas Tech University** *Lubbock, Texas*
7. **University of Kansas** *Lawrence, Kansas*
8. **University of Oklahoma** *Norman, Oklahoma*
9. **University of Texas at Austin** *Austin, Texas*
10. ★ **West Virginia University** *Morgantown, West Virginia*

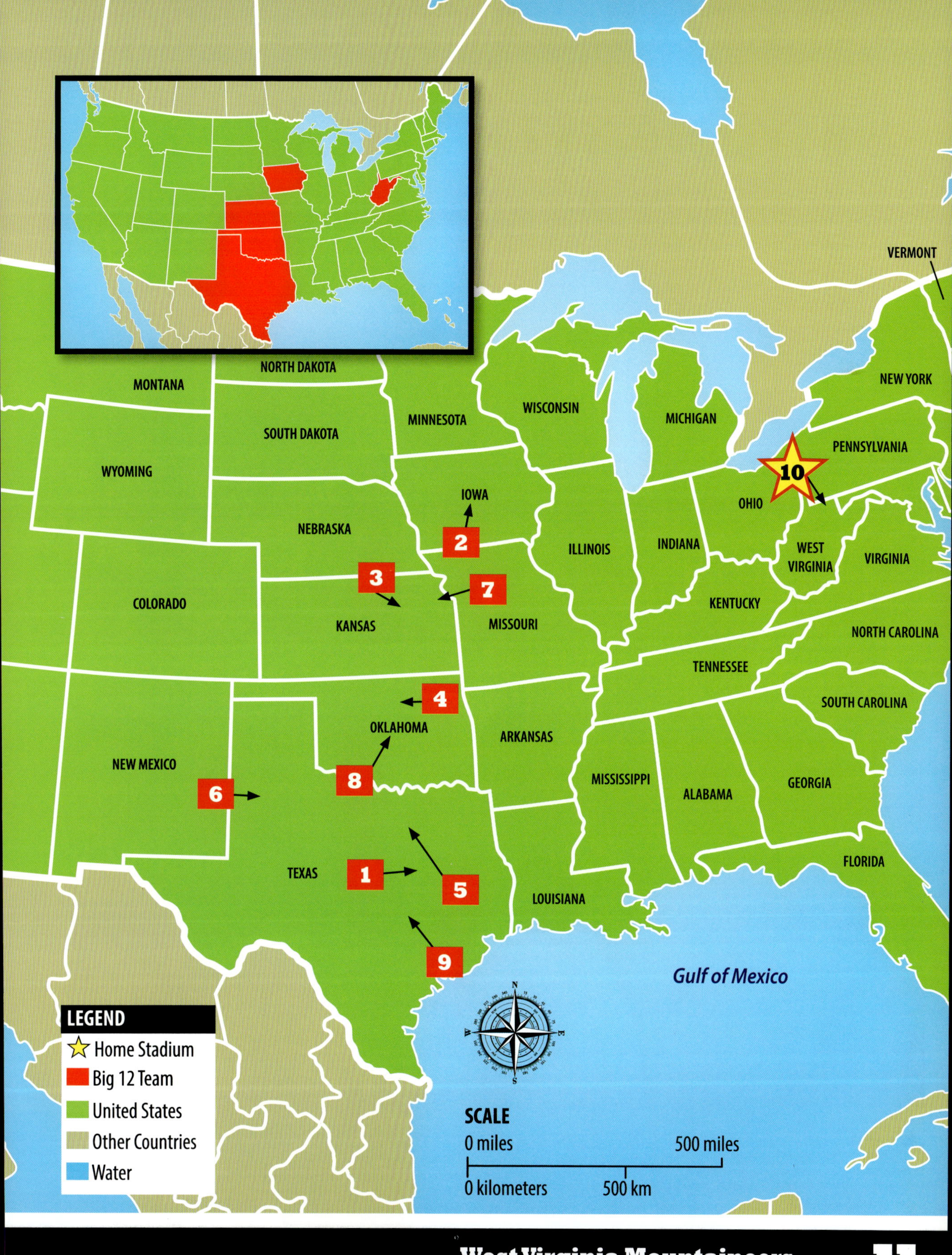
VERMONT
NORTH DAKOTA
MONTANA
NEW YORK
MINNESOTA
WISCONSIN
MICHIGAN
SOUTH DAKOTA
PENNSYLVANIA
WYOMING
10
IOWA
OHIO
NEBRASKA
2
WEST VIRGINIA
ILLINOIS
INDIANA
VIRGINIA
3
7
COLORADO
KENTUCKY
KANSAS
MISSOURI
NORTH CAROLINA
TENNESSEE
4
SOUTH CAROLINA
OKLAHOMA
ARKANSAS
NEW MEXICO
MISSISSIPPI
GEORGIA
8
ALABAMA
6
TEXAS
1
FLORIDA
5
LOUISIANA
9
Gulf of Mexico
LEGEND
Home Stadium
Big 12 Team
United States
Other Countries
Water
SCALE
0 miles
500 miles
0 kilometers
500 km

The Uniforms

The **state-outline logo** was used on helmets through 1979. The team began using it on "throwback" helmets in 2013.

The Mountaineers' 2010 Backyard Brawl uniforms featured a charcoal-colored helmet with a gold "beam of light" down the center that was meant to symbolize the light coming from a coal miner's head gear.

WVU's school colors have been gold and blue since students voted for them in 1890. The main uniform has not changed much since 1980. The team wears gold pants with blue jerseys at home games and white jerseys at away games.

The Mountaineers have worn many interesting alternate uniforms. For example, in the 2010 Backyard Brawl, their uniform honored West Virginia's coal mining industry. The uniform was white and covered with what looked like a layer of coal dust.

The Mountaineers wear blue, gold, or white helmets with a "Flying WV" **logo** on the side. For many years, WVU players wore only a white helmet, but legendary coach Don Nehlen added the blue and gold color scheme because he couldn't tell WVU apart from the other teams in game tape. The shape of the "Flying WV" was inspired by the mountains of West Virginia. It is a very popular logo at the school and across the state.

The Mountaineers' helmets were upgraded in the 2018 season with a three-dimensional bumper on the back that reads "COUNTRY ROADS," a tribute to the John Denver song that players and fans sing after every home win.

Student Athletes

Showtime Camp is an event where WVU's **top recruits** visit campus to spend time with each other and the coaching staff, tour the football facilities, and meet the current team.

West Virginia University's Student-Athlete Enhancement Program provides freshman student athletes such as Trey Lowe III with opportunities to transition to college life, discover career interests, and build relationships with peers and faculty members.

Being a college student athlete is hard work. Student athletes have to perform well on the football field and in the classroom. WVU student athletes generally do very well in school. An average of 50 Mountaineers football players were on the Academic All-Big 12 Team between 2012 and 2018. To help them succeed, student athletes have access to tutoring and mentoring through academic support services.

Many student athletes are given athletic scholarships. An athletic scholarship is a financial aid agreement between the athlete and the college or university. Scholarships are funded by royalties from the famous "Flying WV" logo, ticket sales, and television contracts. Athletes who do not receive an athletic scholarship can be "walk-on" members of the team. This means they are on the team, but without athletic financial aid. West Virginia typically awards the maximum number of football scholarships, which is 85.

David Sills V finished his career with the Mountaineers in 2018 as one of the school's best wide receivers of all time. Sills was listed on the Garrett Ford Academic Honor Roll for WVU student athletes and the Big 12 Commissioner's Honor Roll.

Bowl Games

The Mountaineers had to play the **2006 Sugar Bowl** in Atlanta instead of New Orleans because of the damages caused by Hurricane Katrina.

The Mountaineers defeated the Clemson University Tigers in the 2012 Orange Bowl. West Virginia tied or broke eight team and individual bowl game records during the game, including most touchdowns scored by a team, most points scored by a single player, and most points scored in a half.

After the college football season ends, a rare sports tradition begins. There is no NCAA-sponsored postseason for teams such as the Mountaineers, who are in the Football Bowl Subdivision (FBS). Instead, a variety of games called bowl games are played. There are currently 40 bowl games played between FBS teams. Playing in a bowl game is a chance to compete for respect and wins against rivals. For the top teams, the bowls are also a chance to compete for finalist slots in the FBS-sponsored College Football Playoff National Championship Game that now determines national champions.

The Mountaineers have played in 37 bowls and have a 15–22 bowl record. Their first bowl game was in 1922, when they defeated the Gonzaga University Bulldogs in San Diego, California. They have played in two bowl games that decided the national champions. These games were the Sugar Bowl in 1988 and the Fiesta Bowl in 1993.

Even though West Virginia had a better overall record going into the 2016 Russell Athletic Bowl, the University of Miami Hurricanes were favored to win. The Hurricanes defeated the Mountaineers 31–14.

The Coaches

Don Nehlen holds the WVU record for most bowl games played. He led the team to **13 bowls**.

Neal Brown was named head coach of the Mountaineers in 2019 after four seasons at Troy University. Brown joined the staff at WVU with an overall record of 35–16–0 and three bowl wins.

There have been 33 coaches in WVU history. The first coach was Frederick Lincoln Emory, who had a one-game season that led to a two-year pause in WVU football. The current coach is Neal Brown. In early 2019, Brown took over from Dana Holgorsen, who had coached the Mountaineers since 2011. Brown follows in the footsteps of many great WVU head coaches.

ART "PAPPY" LEWIS Art "Pappy" Lewis put West Virginia football on the map. He was considered an incredible **recruiter**, because he would go anywhere to find players. He even ventured into the mines to find prospects. Lewis won a total of 58 games from 1950 to 1960, including a 30-game Southern Conference winning streak. This streak was a WVU record that lasted 28 years.

DON NEHLEN Don Nehlen brought the team to national recognition, coaching two seasons that ended with the Mountaineers playing in National Championships. He won 149 games from 1980 to 2000. Nehlen coached the most seasons and had the most wins of any WVU coach in the school's history. For all of these distinctions, Nehlen was inducted into the College Football **Hall of Fame**.

RICH RODRIGUEZ Rich Rodriguez's improvement of the team from 2001 to 2002 is the greatest turnaround in Big East history. He won almost 7 out of every 10 games he coached from 2001 to 2007. Rodriguez was named Big East Coach of the Year three times and led WVU to its first consecutive 10-win seasons in school history.

The Mascot

A new student is selected as the Mountaineer each year. The costume is tailored to fit the student playing the mascot. Students who portray the Mountaineer are required to follow a strict code of conduct at all times.

The Mountaineer has been the official mascot of WVU since 1934. Before then, the team was known as the Snakes. The Mountaineer mascot was chosen because West Virginia's state motto is "Mountaineers are always free."

The Mountaineer mascot works nearly every day at games and other events. The mascot wears buckskin clothing and a coonskin cap, and carries a musket that is passed down from student to student. Male Mountaineer mascots usually grow beards. The Mountaineer's musket is a working musket that the mascot uses with gunpowder but without ammunition. The Mountaineer fires the musket while leading the team into the stadium, then fires it again every time WVU scores.

Male and female students can audition to be the Mountaineer, who is chosen by a student committee and a panel of university officials. Since the mascot was introduced in the 1930s, two female students have been chosen to portray the Mountaineer.

Legends of the Past

For many players, their time with the Mountaineers is the start of a promising football career. These are some of the best-known football players to play for West Virginia University.

Sam Huff

Sam Huff is a West Virginia native who was recruited to WVU when a coach came to see another player at his school. He led WVU to a 31–7 record during his four years. He was first-team All-American and first-team Academic All-American. Huff was drafted in the third round by the New York Giants in 1956 and played in the NFL for 13 seasons. Huff had a true love for the game and a great instinct for defense. He was the NFL's top linebacker in 1959. In 1982, he was inducted into the Pro Football Hall of Fame and the College Football Hall of Fame.

Position: Linebacker
Seasons: 1952–1955 (West Virginia Mountaineers), 1956–1963 (New York Giants), 1964–1969 (Washington Redskins)
Born: October 4, 1934, Edna Gas, West Virginia

Marc Bulger

Known for his modesty and work ethic, Marc Bulger is thought of as one of the best quarterbacks in WVU history. When he graduated, he held 25 school records. In 1998, Bulger led the Big East with 3,607 passing yards and 31 touchdowns. Drafted by the New Orleans Saints in the sixth round of the 2000 draft, he ended up with the St. Louis Rams. He had a strong NFL career, with 22,000 passing yards and 122 touchdowns. He was the fifth-fastest quarterback in NFL history to reach 20,000 passing yards. Bulger went to two **Pro Bowls** and was Pro Bowl **Most Valuable Player (MVP)** in 2003. He retired in 2010.

Position: Quarterback
Seasons: 1996–1999 (West Virginia Mountaineers), 2001–2009 (St. Louis Rams), 2010 (Baltimore Ravens)
Born: April 5, 1977, Pittsburgh, Pennsylvania

Pat White

The winningest player in school history, Pat White was a freshman All-American. He was the first quarterback in NCAA history to start and win four bowl games. White was Big East Offensive Player of the Year in 2006 and a 2007 Fiesta Bowl MVP. He is still the single-game and career-total offense leader at WVU, with 10,529 yards. His 34–8 record as a starter and three straight 10-win seasons are unmatched in WVU history. White was drafted in the second round in 2009 by the Miami Dolphins. White retired from professional football in 2015 after an injury, missed seasons, and one year with a pro team in Canada.

Position: Quarterback
Seasons: 2005–2008 (West Virginia Mountaineers), 2009 (Miami Dolphins), 2014 (Canadian Football League Edmonton Eskimos)
Born: February 25, 1986, Daphne, Alabama

Steve Slaton

Steve Slaton played with Pat White. A consensus All-American in 2006, Slaton holds several school and conference records. He scored five rushing touchdowns and a receiving touchdown in a comeback game against the University of Louisville in 2005. This is a Big East record. Slaton was National Player of the Week for that game. The next year, he scored three touchdowns and ran 204 yards for a Sugar Bowl record. His 204 yards were the second-most ever in any Bowl Championship Series game. Slaton was a third-round draft pick in 2008 by the Houston Texans. He played in the NFL for five years.

Position: Running Back
Seasons: 2005–2007 (West Virginia Mountaineers), 2008–2011 (Houston Texans), 2011 (Miami Dolphins)
Born: January 4, 1986, Levittown, Pennsylvania

All-Time Records

502
Average Yards Per Game
The 2012 team holds the record for most yards on average per game in a season, with 502 yards.

55
Career Touchdowns
Steve Slaton scored a record 55 career touchdowns from 2005 to 2007.

16.5
Single-Season Sacks
Canute Curtis holds the Mountaineers record for quarterback sacks in a season, producing 16.5 sacks in 1996.

12,004

Career Passing Yards

Geno Smith holds the WVU record for career passing yards, accounting for 12,004 yards from 2009 to 2012.

384

Career Points

Pat McAfee scored a team record of 384 points during his career from 2005 to 2008.

Timeline

Throughout the team's history, West Virginia University has had many memorable events that have become defining moments for the team and its fans.

In 1952, WVU defeats Pitt under Pappy Lewis. This is the school's first win against a nationally ranked team.

1891
WVU plays its first game against Washington and Jefferson. The team loses 72–0.

1900 | 1920 | 1940 | 1960

1893
The team plays against Mt. Pleasant. It achieves its first win and first shutout.

1924
Mountaineer Field is completed.

1988
The team plays an undefeated regular season.

The Future
The Mountaineers draw thousands of loyal fans to the newly renovated Milan Puskar Stadium every season. Exciting rivalries will continue in 2022 and 2023, when the Backyard Brawl and the series against Penn State return. With state-of-the-art facilities and action-packed games, the team can recruit stronger players. Fans hope this will result in a successful championship season for West Virginia.

2012
WVU joins the Big 12 Conference. Its first game is against the Baylor University Bears, and WVU wins 70–63.

2011
Dana Holgorsen is hired as head coach. The team wins the Big East Conference title.

2019
Neal Brown becomes head coach of the Mountaineers.

1980 | 2000 | 2020

In 1980, the new Mountaineer Field opens with John Denver singing "Take Me Home, Country Roads" before the game.

2016
WVU has its ninth 10-win season in team history, and its first since 2011.

2012
The Mountaineers win the Orange Bowl over Clemson, 70–33. It is a record-setting game.

2000
Don Nehlen retires after 20 years as head coach. His final game is the Music City Bowl against the University of Mississippi, where his team breaks an eight-game bowl losing streak.

Write a Biography

Life Story

A person's life story can be the subject of a book. This kind of book is called a biography. Biographies often describe the lives of people who have achieved great success. These people may be alive today, or they may have lived many years ago. Reading a biography can help you learn more about a great person.

Get the Facts

Use this book, and research in the library and on the internet, to find out more about your favorite player. Learn as much about him as you can. What position does he play? What are his statistics in important categories? Has he set any records? Also, be sure to write down key events in the person's life. What was his childhood like? What has he accomplished off the field? Is there anything else that makes this person special or unusual?

Use the Concept Web

A concept web is a useful research tool. Read the questions in the concept web on the following page. Answer the questions in your notebook. Your answers will help you write a biography.

Concept Web

Adulthood

- Where does this individual currently reside?
- Does he have a family?

Your Opinion

- What did you learn from the books you read in your research?
- Would you suggest these books to others?
- Was anything missing from these books?

Childhood

- Where and when was this person born?
- Describe his parents, siblings, and friends.
- Did he grow up in unusual circumstances?

Accomplishments off the Field

- What is this person's life's work?
- Has he received awards or recognition for accomplishments?
- How have this person's accomplishments served others?

Help and Obstacles

- Did this individual have a positive attitude?
- Did he receive help from others?
- Did this person have a mentor?
- Did this person face any hardships?
- If so, how were the hardships overcome?

Accomplishments on the Field

- What records does he hold?
- What key games and plays have defined his career?
- What are his stats in categories important to his position?

Work and Preparation

- What was this person's education?
- What was his work experience?
- How does this person work?
- What is the process he uses?

Trivia Time

Take this quiz to test your knowledge of the West Virginia Mountaineers. The answers are printed upside down under each question.

1 What conference are the Mountaineers part of?

A. The Big 12 Conference

2 What is the name of WVU's marching band?

A. The Pride of West Virginia

3 What is the name of the team's entrance into the stadium?

A. The "Mountaineer Mantrip"

4 Who does WVU play in the Backyard Brawl?

A. The University of Pittsburgh, or Pitt

5 Which coach was known for his recruiting?

A. Art "Pappy" Lewis

6 Which Mountaineers coach is in the College Football Hall of Fame?

A. Don Nehlen

7 Which WVU player was inducted into the Pro Football Hall of Fame in 1982?

A. Sam Huff

8 Who is the winningest player in Mountaineers history?

A. Pat White

9 What was the first year of WVU football?

A. 1891

10 What was WVU's first team name?

A. The Snakes

Key Words

All-Americans: players, usually in high school or college, judged to be the best in each position of a sport

draft: an annual event where the NFL chooses college football players to be new team members

Hall of Fame: a group of persons judged to be outstanding in a particular sport

legends: extremely well-known or famous people

logo: a symbol that stands for a team or organization

Most Valuable Player (MVP): the player judged to be most valuable to his team's success

Pro Bowls: the annual all-star games for NFL players pitting the best players in the National Football Conference against the best players in the American Football Conference

recruiter: a person who works to enroll someone as a member of an organization

renovation: construction that works to improve or expand an older building

rivalries: competitions between different groups or individuals toward the same objective or goal

Index

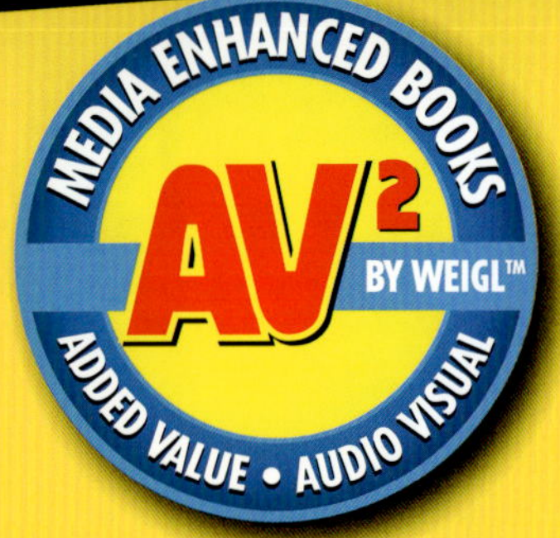

Log on to www.av2books.com

AV² by Weigl brings you media enhanced books that support active learning. Go to www.av2books.com, and enter the special code found on page 2 of this book. You will gain access to enriched and enhanced content that supplements and complements this book. Content includes video, audio, weblinks, quizzes, a slideshow, and activities.

AV² Online Navigation

Audio
Listen to sections of the book read aloud.

Book Pages
AV² pages directly correspond to pages in the book.

Video
Watch informative video clips.

Embedded Weblinks
Gain additional information for research.

Key Words
Study vocabulary, and complete a matching word activity.

Try This!
Complete activities and hands-on experiments.

Quizzes
Test your knowledge.

Slideshow
View images and captions, and prepare a presentation.

AV² was built to bridge the gap between print and digital. We encourage you to tell us what you like and what you want to see in the future.

Sign up to be an AV² Ambassador at www.av2books.com/ambassador.

Due to the dynamic nature of the internet, some of the URLs and activities provided as part of AV² by Weigl may have changed or ceased to exist. AV² by Weigl accepts no responsibility for any such changes. All media enhanced books are regularly monitored to update addresses and sites in a timely manner. Contact AV² by Weigl at 1-866-649-3445 or av2books@weigl.com with any questions, comments, or feedback.